WHAT ON EARTH IS A
PANGOLIN

?

EDWARD R. RICCIUTI

A BLACKBIRCH PRESS BOOK

WOODBRIDGE, CONNECTICUT

Published by Blackbirch Press, Inc.
One Bradley Road, Suite 104
Woodbridge, CT 06525

©1994 Blackbirch Press, Inc.
First Edition

Printed in Hong Kong

10 9 8 7 6 5 4 3 2 1

Photo Credits

Cover and title page: ©Roland Seitre/Peter Arnold, Inc.
Pages 4—5: ©Roland Seitre/ Peter Arnold, Inc.; page 6 (top left): ©Roland Seitre/Peter
Arnold, Inc., (top right): ©Mandal Ranjih/Photo Researchers, Inc., (bottom): ©G.L.
Kooyman/Animals Animals; page 7: ©E. Hanumantha Rao/Photo Researchers, Inc; page 9:
©G.L. Kooyman/Animals Animals; pages 10—11: ©Roland Seitre/ Peter Arnold, Inc.; page
13: ©Roland Seitre/ Peter Arnold, Inc.; pages 14—15: ©Roland Seitre/ Peter Arnold, Inc.;
page17: ©Roland Seitre/ Peter Arnold, Inc.; page 19: ©Stouffer Prod. Ltd./Animals
Animals; page 20: ©Roland Seitre/ Peter Arnold, Inc.; pages 22—23 ©Roland Seitre/ Peter
Arnold, Inc.; page 25: ©Roland Seitre/ Peter Arnold, Inc.; page 26: ©Roland Seitre/ Peter
Arnold, Inc.; page 29: ©Roland Seitre/ Peter Arnold, Inc.

Library of Congress Cataloging-in-Publication Data
Ricciuti, Edward R.
What on earth is a pangolin? / by Edward R. Ricciuti. — 1st ed.
    p.   cm. — (What on earth series)
    Includes bibliographical references (p.   ) and index.
    ISBN 1-56711-090-8
    1. Pangolins—Juvenile literature. [1. Pangolins.   2. Mammals.]
I. Title.   II. Series.
QL737.P4R53   1994
599.3'1—dc20   94-22517
                                                                    CIP
                                                                    AC

What does it look like?

Where does it live?

What does it eat?

How does it reproduce?

How does it survive?

TURN THESE PAGES AND FIND OUT!

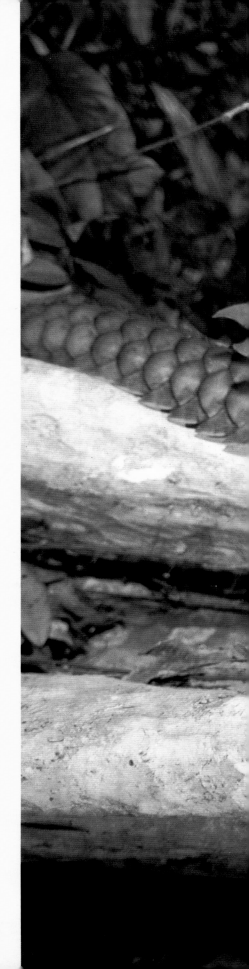

A pangolin is an animal that looks like a cross between an anteater and an armadillo. Its body is covered in hard, flat scales. Its long snout helps it to find small insects to eat on the ground.

A PANGOLIN'S BODY IS COVERED WITH LAYERS OF FLAT, HARD SCALES.

LEFT: A MALAYAN PANGOLIN.
BELOW: AN INDIAN PANGOLIN.
BOTTOM: A CHINESE PANGOLIN.

Pangolins are mammals, like elephants, dogs, rats, and humans. They give birth to live young and suckle them while they are small. As a group, mammals are what wildlife scientists call a "class" of animals. Other classes include birds, reptiles, and fishes. Scientists divide each class into smaller groups called "orders."

Pangolins belong to an order that contains only them. There are just seven kinds, or species, of pangolins—the giant pangolin, Cape pangolin, small-scaled tree pangolin, log-tailed pangolin, Indian pangolin, Chinese pangolin, and Malayan pangolin.

SOME PANGOLINS CLIMB TREES IN SEARCH OF INSECTS TO EAT.

Scientists call the pangolin order Pholidota.
This name comes from ancient Greek words that
mean "wearing scales." The name fits. A pangolin
looks like a walking pine cone because most of its
body is covered with large, hard scales. The flat
scales overlap like roof shingles and are made of
material similar to human fingernails. The edges
are very sharp and a pangolin can raise or lower
its scales. When old scales fall off, new ones
grow to replace them. There are no scales on a
pangolin's snout, face, throat, belly, or inner sides
of its legs. These areas are fleshy and hairy.

THIS DETAIL OF A CHINESE PANGOLIN'S
BACK SHOWS HOW THE FLAT SCALES
OVERLAP TO COVER THE BODY.

Pangolins come in a variety of sizes. The long-tailed pangolin is the smallest species. It is about 3 feet (1 meter) long and weighs 3 or 4 pounds (about 2 kilograms). The biggest is the giant pangolin. It is almost 6 feet (2 meters) long and can weigh more than 70 pounds (about 32 kilograms).

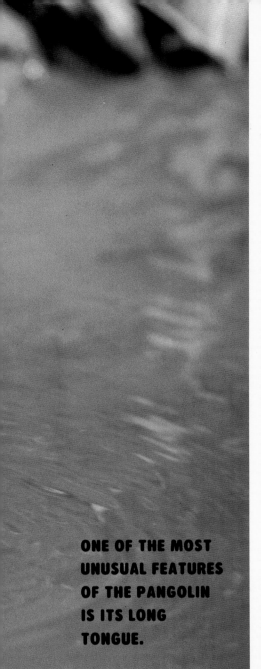

ONE OF THE MOST
UNUSUAL FEATURES
OF THE PANGOLIN
IS ITS LONG
TONGUE.

Pangolins have five large, curved claws on each foot. The three middle claws on each front foot grow up to 9 inches (23 centimeters) long. When walking on all fours, the toes are turned under. When they walk, pangolins look as if they are traveling on their knuckles. When on all fours, pangolins move slowly. If one is in a hurry, it stands up, using its tail for support, and runs at a speed of up to 3 miles (5 kilometers) an hour.

Another interesting feature of the pangolin is its large tongue, which is unusually long. The giant pangolin's tongue can reach a length of about 2 feet (61 centimeters)! It can also reach more than 1 foot (30 centimeters) from the animal's mouth. Gooey saliva coats the tongue. The saliva is produced by a huge gland inside the pangolin's chest. Even more amazing, muscles connect the tongue of a pangolin to bones all the way back in its hip area.

Pangolins live in climates that range from warm to hot. Giant pangolins, Cape pangolins, tree pangolins, and long-tailed pangolins live in Africa. Other species are found in southern Asia. Rainforests are the home of the tree pangolin and long-tailed pangolin. They spend most of their time high up in the trees. Like some monkeys, these pangolins have tails that help them climb by grasping branches.

Climbing pangolins sleep in trees. Other species rest in burrows in the ground and under tree roots. Some burrows dug by pangolins are more than 100 feet (31 meters) long. Except for the long-tailed pangolins, most species feed at night and sleep during the day.

China

AFRICA

India

Taiwan

Pacific Ocean

Malaysia

Indian Ocean

Sumatra

Atlantic Ocean

Java

WHERE PANGOLINS ARE FOUND

SOME SPECIES OF PANGOLINS SPEND MOST OF THEIR TIME IN TREES.

IN ADDITION TO CLIMBING
TREES AND WALKING ON
LAND, MOST PANGOLINS ARE
ALSO GOOD SWIMMERS.

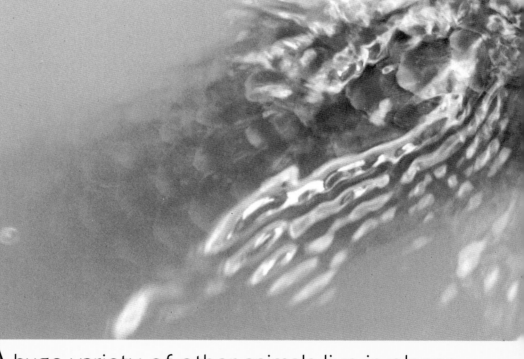

A huge variety of other animals live in places
inhabited by pangolins. On the African plains,
pangolins live with elephants, lions, hyenas,
baboons, antelope, eagles, hawks, and ostriches.
In drier areas of southern Africa, pangolins

sometimes compete for food with animals such as aardwolves and aardvarks.

In Asia, some pangolins live in tiger country and share their surroundings with monkeys, elephants, and many birds and rodents.

Pangolins are sometimes called "scaly anteaters" because they feed on ants and termites. In one night, a pangolin may eat 200,000 insects! For protection against biting ants, the pangolin can close its nostrils and ear openings. It also has very thick eyelids for protection.

The ants and termites that pangolins like to eat make large nests. The walls of these nests are hard as plaster but the pangolin's large claws can easily tear through them. Once the walls are opened, the pangolin slips its tongue into passages running through the nest and laps up the insects with its sticky tongue.

Pangolins do not have teeth and cannot chew their food. Instead, their food is ground up by the hard, rough walls of their stomach, and by tiny pebbles that they swallow.

PANGOLINS OFTEN BURROW INTO THE GROUND TO FEED ON ANTS AND
TERMITES THAT BUILD THEIR NESTS IN THE SOIL.

Most places inhabited by pangolins are also home to leopards and python snakes, some of which grow very large. Both sometimes kill and eat pangolins.

Few other creatures besides leopards and pythons eat pangolins. This is because the pangolin's scales are a very prickly defense. When attacked, a pangolin rolls up with its tail wrapped tightly around its body. It then raises its sharp-edged scales. In this position, its soft underside is shielded from attack. It is very hard for a predator to get past the pangolin's armor. Even an adult human cannot unroll a pangolin once it is coiled!

Pangolins also have a few other means of self-defense. One scientist saw a frightened pangolin coil up, then roll down a hill. It covered more than 90 feet (27 meters) in 10 seconds! Pangolins will also squirt their enemies with a smelly liquid from glands in their rear. They may even urinate on an animal that threatens them! Because pangolins are good swimmers, they sometimes go into the water to escape danger.

WHEN A PANGOLIN IS THREATENED, IT WILL ROLL ITSELF UP INTO A TIGHT BALL. PANGOLINS CAN ROLL THEMSELVES SO TIGHTLY THAT EVEN LARGE PREDATORS CANNOT UNCOIL THEM.

Pangolins generally live alone, except for short periods when males and females mate. Each pangolin has a territory within which it lives. Male territories can be up to 63 acres (20 hectares) in size. Female territories are no more than 10 acres (4 hectares). A pangolin marks the borders of its territory with urine and the same smelly liquid it uses to defend itself. Other pangolins that smell this will usually stay away from a marked area. Scientists think that, during the mating season, the scents probably also bring males and females together.

PANGOLINS MARK THEIR TERRITORIES
BY SECRETING URINE OR A SMELLY
LIQUID ON TREES AND BUSHES.

A BABY PANGOLIN CRAWLS ON TOP OF ITS RESTING, TIGHTLY CURLED MOTHER.

Pangolins are ready to mate when they are about two years old. A pair of pangolins usually produces one offspring at a time. When pangolins mate, the male places sperm inside the female by inserting his penis into her vagina. The sperm then joins with an egg inside the female. The result is fertilization and an "embryo," which is a new, developing organism. A pangolin embryo grows and develops inside the female for about five months before it is born. The babies are usually born between November and March.

At birth, a young pangolin weighs between 7 and 18 ounces (about 340 grams). Its scales are soft and do not overlap, but they harden in a day and soon grow larger. A mother pangolin pays close attention to her young. When sleeping or frightened, she curls around her baby. When she travels about, the youngster rides on her tail or back, holding on to her scales with its claws. Females sometimes adopt other young that have lost their real mother.

A young pangolin feeds on its mother's milk for three months. Then it begins to eat the ants it finds crawling on its mother's scales. Five months after birth, the young pangolin leaves its mother and starts to live on its own.

PANGOLIN MOTHERS TAKE GOOD CARE OF THEIR YOUNG DURING THE
FIRST MONTHS OF A BABY'S LIFE. FOR PROTECTION, A MOTHER WILL
CURL HERSELF AROUND HER BABY TO SHIELD IT.

IN MANY PARTS OF AFRICA
AND ASIA, PANGOLINS ARE
CAPTURED BY HUMANS FOR
FOOD AND FOR THEIR HIDES
AND SCALES.

Pangolins are becoming rare in a number of
locations due to human activities. In both Africa
and Asia, many people consider pangolins very
good to eat. Because of this, large numbers of
pangolins are killed for food.

Pangolin scales and hides are also worth a
good deal of money. Many Asian and African
peoples believe that crushed pangolin scales are
a powerful medicine against disease. Pangolin
hides have been used instead of leather in many
countries, including the United States. Hundreds
of thousands of pangolins have been destroyed
so their scales and hides could be sold.

The Cape pangolin is the least-common kind of pangolin. It is also in danger of extinction. It has been heavily hunted for its scales, and its habitat has been destroyed, largely for agriculture. It has been poisoned by dangerous pesticides that are used on farm crops.

Habitat destruction also threatens other pangolins, especially those living in forests. Large areas of African and Asian forests are being cut for lumber and for real estate development. When the forests are destroyed, the pangolins—and other forest-dwelling animals—have no place to live. Without a place to live, a plant or animal will eventually become extinct. For pangolins, losing their forest habitats means they will eventually disappear.

DESTRUCTION OF FOREST HABITATS IN AFRICA AND ASIA HAS THREATENED THE EXISTENCE OF PANGOLINS. TO PROTECT THESE UNIQUE CREATURES, HUMANS MUST TAKE CARE TO PRESERVE THE LAND ON WHICH PANGOLINS DEPEND.

Glossary

egg Female sex cell.

embryo The young organism developing within the egg.

extinct No longer in existence.

fertilize The union of sperm and egg that creates a new organism.

habitat Surroundings that provide an animal with space, shelter, and food.

mammals A group of animals, including people, that produce their own body heat, have hair, and feed their young on milk.

nostrils The openings to the nasal passages.

predator An animal that hunts other animals for food.

scales Hard, flat body features that overlap to protect the outside of an animal's body.

sperm Male sex cell.

territory An area in which an animal lives, feeds, and mates.

For Further Reading

Aldis, Rodney. *Rainforests*. New York: Dillon, 1991.

Chinery, Michael. *Rainforest Animals*. New York: Random Books for Young Readers, 1992.

Ganeri, Anita. *Small Mammals*. Chicago: Watts, 1993.

Lambert, David. *The Golden Concise Encyclopedia of Mammals*. New York: Western, 1992.

Munan, Heidi. *Malaysia*. Bellmore, NY: Marshall Cavendish, 1991.

Nurland, Patricia. *Vietnam*. Milwaukee: Gareth Stevens, 1991.

Parsons, Alexandra. *Amazing Mammals*. New York: Random House, 1990.

Tangley, Laura. *Rainforest*. New York: Chelsea House, 1992.

Tesar, Jenny. *Mammals*. Woodbridge, CT: Blackbirch Press, Inc., 1993.

The Sierra Club Book of Small Mammals. San Francisco: Sierra, 1993.

Warburton, Lois. *Rainforests*. San Diego: Lucent, 1991.

Index